All scriptures quotations not marked (NLT) are taken from the Authorized King James Version of the Bible.

ISBN-13: 9798992148305

Printed in the United States of America

CONTENTS

ACKNOWLEDGEMENTS

I want to thank the Most High, My Father Jehovah, and my LORD and Savior, Jesus Christ. Without the grace, mercy, and favor I receive from them daily; I would be caught by the snares the enemy tries to set up for me. For when I was a child, I was writing books, poetry, songs, and short plays. But in my twenties, I stopped writing and lost my way. I did not know what my purpose was on earth, and I was suffering because of it. I often wondered why some people seem to have it all while I was stuck in a cycle of depression and frustration. But as I continue to grow in faith, God reminded me of my gifts and with any gift, it's expected to be used to benefit his kingdom.

After my brother passed, I started thinking about all I ever wanted was to become an author and what a shame if I was to leave this world without having written one book. Therefore, as I started contemplating on what to write about, I started discussing with my cousin, Kayla McPhearson, my desires to let people who are suffering know how they can have victory in their lives. She said it was a great idea, and people needed a book like this one. At that point, I started writing and therefore present to you a "Deliverance Manual for Everyone not Just the Believer", dedicated to my deceased brother, Antonio Ray Dabney Christian.

INTRODUCTION

In this book, I hope to not only inspire you to overcome the challenges that you are facing but also help others who need help as well. This manual includes chapters on deliverance which discuss before, during, and after a deliverance session. It has prayers backed with scripture and true stories of the things that I witnessed or faced over the years. In addition to scriptures, there are plenty of tips to help you achieve victory if you are a non-believer. My prayer for ever reader is that you know sickness, poverty, and mental illness are not your portion.

MY SPIRITUAL JOURNEY FOR DELIVERANCE

I wish someone told me that if you don't fully commit to living a life of repentance and meditate on God's word after getting baptized that I would have more problems than I had before I got saved (Matthew 12:43-45).

I decided to be baptized in a church at 28 years old. I was going to church regularly, and I thought I was ready to turn my life around. The night I was baptized, I didn't feel any change. I was very disappointed. I was thinking, *I don't feel any different.* Where is the special feeling I'm supposed to have? But the next day was the happiest day of my life. I woke up feeling extremely light. I felt as if I didn't have an ounce of sin in me. I was extremely happy. I had a spiritual glow. At work, people treated me different. Instead of being the party girl and everyone waiting for me to talk about my escapades, I was treated with respect and people were mindful of how they spoke to me. Everyone was so nice back then. I don't know if they changed, or if it was the way I perceived things. The one guy that I was messing around with kept implying that he was happy for me, and he was okay with me not being with him, but he was just baiting me. Weeks later, I ended up back in bed with him, which led to condemnation, guilt, and depression!

Giving Praise:

Father God, I thank you for taking me out of the enemy's hands. Throughout the years, I was partying every weekend and crying every night. You were there! You were there when the waters were about to take me under when I was younger. You were there when the enemy tried to take me out via several car accidents. You were there each time I was given items or food that was used to afflict me with witchcraft! You were there every time I was lied to or plotted against. You were there! You were there every time I had horrific nightmares and was scared to fall asleep by myself. You were there! You were there every time I was violated, molested, harassed, and tormented. You were there! You were there the whole time during the good and the bad, waiting for me to follow your commandments, develop an intimate relationship with you, and speak your will over my life. You were waiting on me to seek you! And now that I have found you, I vow that we are forever bonded together, in Jesus' mighty name, I pray. Amen.

WHY DO YOU NEED DELIVERANCE?

<u>You Have Open Doors for the Enemy</u>

Adulatery Bitterness Curses False Religion Familiar Spirts Fornication Idol Worship Incest Masturbation Necromancy Mediums New Age Occult Offense Pornography Pride Psychics Rebellion Resentment Sexual Perversion Trauma Unforgiveness Yoga Witchcraft

For the longest time, the 3 things that I enjoyed the most was food, sex, and sleep. God allowed Satan to attack me in each of these areas because these were strongholds that I needed to get rid of. For every time you transgress or sin, it creates a corresponding demonic connection giving the devil legal right to enter our lives. The book of Deuteronomy 28 contains many curses that one can experience such as humiliation, barrenness, sickness, poverty, failure, defeat, helplessness, weaknesses, and death.

These curses begin to form in the spirit realm, and without challenge and rebuke, they will show up in the physical realm. In Romans 1:20 says, "For the invisible things of him from the creation of the world are clearly seen, being understood by the things that are made, even his eternal power and Godhead."

God gave man dominion in the earth and physical realm in Genesis 1:26, but when Adam and Eve sin, Satan got dominion temporarily until Jesus came and took the keys from the enemy and passed that same power to us in Matthew 28:18.

A combination of God's word, the name and blood of Jesus, fasting, praise and worship, or speaking in holy tongues are all tools that believers can use in spiritual warfare.

Because the devil's job is for the saints to become weary and change themselves to not look like God's creation. He wants as many souls as possible to join him and the rest of the fallen angels in hell. You must stand tall in Jesus Christ and know he will not allow more than you can stand. Declare your dominion over serpents and scorpions speak God's word over your life every day, not the new age term "affirmations" but God's word, to achieve the victory and the life of abundance that God intended for you to have.

For we can do all things through Jesus Christ who strengthens us, so therefore not only do we need to rely on Jesus every day but pray without ceasing.

Pastor Stephen Darby said, "Satan is an abortionist. He wants you to give up on your blessing through disobedience, rebellion, and laziness. If you currently have problems praying or reading your Bible, find someone to be an intercessor for you to help bind those mind binding spirits.

If you need help identifying evil spirits, there's a list of demons and their characteristics in Apostle John Eckhardt's book, *Demon Hit List.*

STARTING YOUR DELIVERANCE JOURNEY

"Before I formed thee in the belly I knew thee; and before thou camest forth out of the womb I sanctified thee, and I ordained thee a prophet unto the nations." (Jeremiah 1:5)

"What? know ye not that your body is the temple of the Holy Ghost which is in you, which ye have of God, and ye are not your own? For ye are bought with a price: therefore glorify God in your body, and in your spirit, which are God's." (1 Corinthians 6:19-20)

Before reading your Bible, repent of your sins as in Psalm 66:18 so there will be no iniquity in your heart. Normally, when you have daily conversation with the LORD, you pray in silence (Matthew 6:6), but when praising God, engaging in spiritual warfare, or asking for forgiveness of your sins this must be done. Let the enemy know that he is a defeated foe because you have accepted Jesus Christ as your LORD and Savior, and Christ is the head of all principalities and powers in accordance with Colossians 2:10.

So, how do you know what sins you need to confess and ask for forgiveness? First, look at your family history. What cycle of negative things are happening on both sides of your family. For example, my family has generational curses of incest, addiction, rape, molestation, sorcery, divination, witchcraft, poverty, diabetes, high blood pressure, cancer, fornication, adultery, pride, rebellion, rejection, and offense. For not only do you have to repent of your sins but those of your ancestors. There are several examples of generation blessings and curses in the Holy Bible, which is God's word. You must break those curses to see the real blessings for what God intended for you to have.

Next, pray through the Holy Spirt and write down the things that you are plagued with and/or have wrongly engaged with in the past and present.

Confess these things as well as ask for forgiveness of sins known and unknown. Be mindful that any unforgiveness in your heart towards anyone must be confessed as well.

It's best to not seek deliverance if you have resentment, bitterness, or unforgiveness. Deal with these areas first by repenting and asking for forgiveness because the LORD will not hear you with iniquity in your heart (Psalm 66:18). More about these sins are in Chapter 10 and Chapter 26, but once you turn your attention to the true enemy and realize they are being used for the enemy agenda. You will start to feel sorry for them for they are truly lost.

"But without faith it is impossible to please him: for he that cometh to God must believe that he is, and that he is a rewarder of them that diligently seek him" (Hebrews 11:6).

According to Pastor Kevin LA Ewing, "Faith to God is equivalent to money in our society for goods and services." Now faith is the substance of things hoped for, the evidence of things not seen (Hebrews 11:11).

In the Bible, there are plenty of examples of how faith can move you towards your blessing, so increase your faith by starting off by reading Hebrews Chapter 11.

Prayer Point:

Father God, I believe Jesus Christ died on the cross and through him I ask for forgiveness for ______________ and my sins unknown for I am redeemed through his innocent blood. I pray that I am led by the Holy Spirt as I seek to build my relationship with you. I renounce and rebuke all covenants with Satan's kingdom, and I declare my body is the temple of the Holy Ghost for I was bought with a price. Father, let the blood of Jesus purify and cleanse my mind, body, soul, and spirit as I declare your word in Jeremiah 29:11 that your thoughts for me are to provide me with peace and an expected end. In Jesus' mighty name, I pray. Amen

(IN THE SPACE, ANNOUNCE YOUR SINS)

GET YOUR HOUSE IN ORDER

"And thou shalt take the anointing oil, and anoint the tabernacle, and all that is therein, and shalt hallow it, and all the vessels thereof: and it shall be holy." (Exodus 40:9)

Pray for God to reveal cursed objects so you can destroy or remove them. Don't focus on the cost or where or who you received the items from! Why hold on to something that is cursing your life?

If you committed any sin such as witchcraft, get rid of those items as they are cursed. Get some extra virgin olive oil and pray God's word for a hedge of protection around you, your family, and everyone who enters your home. Pray the scriptures out loud as you anoint all doors and windows, including cabinets and absolutely do not use sage or incense, as they are what witches used to perform rituals against you.

If someone from the occult gave you something, throw it away immediately. Unless you are a 100% sure they served Jesus Christ of Nazareth, don't keep any gifts, especially from those in your workplace.

Look around your home for demonic paintings, items used for witchcraft, statues of gods, rosaries, candles used for rituals, horoscope and astrology paraphernalia, fortune telling material, good luck charms, role playing video games, rock & roll, demonic rap, and/or soul music. Also look for pagan, Jehovah Witness, Catholic, Islam, Mason or Occult material.

Prayer Point:

I command anything from the kingdom of Satan that has been inhabiting this place to go, in the name of Jesus. I command all the legal rights that have been given to the kingdom of darkness to stay to be broken, in the name of Jesus. I command all associated curses, incantations, and covenants to be broken now, in the name of Jesus. Every evil spirit living in this location, leave this place now and never return, in the name of Jesus. I dedicate and call on the peace of God to rule and reign in my home in Jesus' name. Father God, I ask You to cleanse my home by the power of the Holy Spirit, in the name of Jesus. Oh LORD, saturate my home inside and out with the blood of Jesus Christ. Provide me with a hedge of protection as you did around Job. For I proclaim this place holy unto the LORD as in Exodus [illegible]0:29, as I dedicate it to the LORD Jesus of Nazareth, Amen.

*Maintain the protection of your home by praying daily especially when anyone visits your home.

ADDICTION OR YOUR CROSS TO BEAR

Alcohol **Fetish** **Food** **Gambling**
Gluttony **Masturbation** **Nicotine** **Drugs**
Pornography **Promiscuous** **Prostitution** **Sexual Fantasy**
Spendthrift

Satan knows the areas where you are weak, so he will always try to tempt you in them. For example, unresolved trauma can cause someone to develop unhealthy coping mechanisms, like being promiscuous. Habitually smoking weed opens your natural mind, and when you stop getting high, the demons torment you with depressing thoughts. Being greedy or excessively consuming food or sugary drinks, causes you to become obese by eating poorly. These addictions along with many others show you need to take control of your flesh and bring it into subjection. By overindulging, you are causing the demons to get stronger.

Scriptures:

"Blessed is the man that endureth temptation: for when he is tried, he shall receive the crown of life, which the LORD hath promised to them that love him. Let no man say when he is tempted, I am tempted of God: for God cannot be tempted with evil, neither tempteth he any man: But every man is tempted, when he is drawn away of his own lust, and enticed. Then when lust hath conceived, it bringeth forth sin: and sin, when it is finished, bringeth forth death." (James 1:12-15)

"There hath no temptation taken you but such as is common to man: but God is faithful, who will not suffer you to be tempted above that ye are able; but will with the temptation also make a way to escape, that ye may be able to bear it." (1 Corinthians 10:13)

"Dear brothers and sisters, if another believer is overcome by some sin, you who are godly should gently and humbly help that person back onto the right path. And be careful not to fall into the same temptation yourself." (Galatians 6:1 NLT)

In Pastor Stephen Darby's sermon called "Pornography," lust is never satisfied. As you continue to give in to sexual lust, you become more desensitized and become more perverted i.e. getting involved in homosexuality, incest, pedophilia, rape, killing, or bestiality. Your spouse becomes less attractive as you continue to try to fulfill your lustful desires.

Prayer Point:

Father God, I declare your word that my body is a temple of the Holy Spirit, and it was bought with a price. I renounce and rebuke the spirits of ________ and__________ in my life. Every ______________, ______________, ______________. I bind you demons on earth and in heaven, and I send you straight to the abyss. I send the Holy Ghost fire to destroy all evidence of these evil spirits in my life. Father, let me rely on the escape route to avoid temptation as in 1 Corinthians 10:13, as well as to know that you are watching me, for nothing shall be hidden from you. In Jesus' mighty name, I pray. Amen.

RENOUNCE AND REBUKE THE SINS YOU ARE DEALING WITH

Actionable Steps:

If gambling is your problem, begin by only taking a certain amount of money with you and absolutely no credit cards. Keep a journal of how much money you spent and how much you return home with after leaving the casino. Make it a point to journal about it. At the end of month look at the total spent versus won at the casino. Is there a significant difference? Do you have better usage for the money? Could that money have been used to save for a vacation? Pay off a credit card? Make double payments on your car note, buy new clothes or go to a fancy restaurant? Or, help someone in need, thereby unlocking the keys to financial blessings.

If you have a sex addition, stop watching or listening to anything involving sex. Get rid of all books or paraphernalia. Avoid hanging out or talking to anyone that you find attractive. Make sure your home is free from anything you use (beside your bed) for your sexual escapades). {You might need to get a new mattress, though} Pray to God to help you remove the spirit of lust and ensure you repent from every sin. Declare that God can deliver you out of anything, so you know he can deliver you from the spirit of lust. Also, read chapter 22 because you may have a spirit spouse that you need to get rid of too.

I personally did this after I decided I didn't want to be with women anymore. I finally had a real talk with God. I said I don't understand when someone says they believe in God to heal them from cancer and diabetes, but they can't be delivered from homosexuality. Right then, I said, "no more", and I started cleaning the house. I stopped hanging out with certain people, and I got rid of everything that I had from the women I was crushing on. I got rid of all pornography movies, and I stopped watching all shows that either had gay or homosexual characters or had people who I was attracted to on their show. God saw that I was serious and before I knew it, the homosexual spirit was gone. This was about 20 years ago and I never backslide. Now, from time to time, the enemy tries to get me to look at a particular person, but I don't pay the devil no mind because I declare I am free from that sin.

Note: The celebrities that I was attracted to back them, I still do not watch them on television. I will not open the door for the enemy to tempt me. In addition, I ask God to remove the spirit of lust, for I would rather not have any sexual desire than to go back to fornication. God answered my prayers so that when I feel a strong sexual desire, I know that a warlock or warlocks are trying to project it on me. At that point, I declare my body is a temple of the Holy Spirit, and I bind every spirit of lust, adultery, and fornication. I declare God's word: he shall destroy anything that defiles or try to defile the temple of the Holy Spirit, for my body does not belong to me.

If gluttony from food is your problem, you need to fast at least once a week. Buffet your flesh to bring it under submission. Set a time every day that you will absolutely have nothing else to eat. Repeat to yourself that you will not let your stomach be your God.

If you have problems with masturbation, take the same steps as the sex addiction, as well as constantly reminding yourself that every time you defile (masturbate), you are feeding demons. The demons are gaining more control over your flesh. This will cause you severe health problems eventually. When you go to bed either combine your hands together as if you are praying or keep something in your hand.

This will serve as a reminder to not masturbate and to keep your hands pure and holy. Also, remember you can't hide from God and the tingling in your hands is judgement.

If you have a problem with using profanity, pay attention to your environment, are you watching shows with profanity in them? Are you listening to music or videos with profanity in them? Are you around people who use profanity? Are you reading articles, comments, or memes that have cursing in them? These are where that profanity spirit gain its momentum. You stop engaging in these items along with trying to stop using profanity yourself, and I guarantee you will no longer have a cursing problem.

FEELING LOST- NEED ADVICE/GUIDANCE

The first rule is don't seek advice from carnal minded people.

"Blessed is the man that walketh not in the counsel of the ungodly, nor standeth in the way of sinners, nor sitteth in the seat of the scornful. But his delight is in the law of the LORD; and in his law doth he meditates day and night. And he shall be like a tree planted by the rivers of water, that bringeth forth his fruit in his season; his leaf also shall not wither; and whatsoever he doeth shall prosper." (Psalms 1:1-3)

Scriptures:

"Asking God, the glorious Father of our LORD Jesus Christ, to give you spiritual wisdom and insight so that you might grow in your knowledge of God." (Ephesians 1:17 NLT)

"If any of you lack wisdom, let him ask of God, that giveth to all men liberally, and upbraideth not; and it shall be given him." (James 1:5)

"A wise man is strong; yea, a man of knowledge increaseth strength." (Proverbs 24:5)

"Ask, and it shall be given you; seek, and ye shall find; knock, and it shall be opened unto you: For everyone that asketh receiveth; and he that seeketh findeth; and to him that knocketh it shall be opened." (Matthew 7:7-8)

"But when he, the Spirit of truth, comes, he will guide you into all the truth. He will not speak on his own; he will speak only what he hears, and he will tell you what is yet to come." (John 16:13 NIV)

“My people are destroyed for lack of knowledge: because thou hast rejected knowledge, I will also reject thee, that thou shalt be no priest to me: seeing thou hast forgotten the law of thy God, I will also forget thy children.” (Hosea 4:6)

“Very truly, I tell you, whoever believes in me will do the works I have been doing, and they will do even greater things than these, because I am going to the Father. And I will do whatever you ask in my name, so that the Father may be glorified in the Son. You may ask me for anything in my name, and I will do it.” (John 14:12-14 NIV)

“I will make them and the places surrounding my hill a blessing. I will send down showers in season; there will be showers of blessing.” (Ezekiel 34:26 NIV)

“I will instruct you and teach you in the way you should go; I will counsel you with my loving eye on you.” (Psalm 32:8 NIV)

"Death and life are in the power of the tongue: and they that love it shall eat the fruit thereof." (Proverbs 18:21)

“But we speak the wisdom of God in a mystery, even the hidden wisdom, which God ordained before the world unto our glory.” (1 Corinthians 2:7)

“Blessed be the God and Father of our LORD Jesus Christ, who hath blessed us with all spiritual blessings in heavenly places in Christ.” (Ephesians 1:3)

“And the spirit of the LORD shall rest upon him, the spirit of wisdom and understanding, the spirit of counsel and might, the spirit of knowledge and of the fear of the LORD.” (Isaiah 11:2)

“That the God of our LORD Jesus Christ, the Father of glory, may give unto you the spirit of wisdom and revelation in the knowledge of him.” (Ephesians 1:17)

"Trust in the LORD with all thine heart; and lean not unto thine own understanding." (Proverbs 3:5)

“Now unto him that is able to do exceeding abundantly above all that we ask or think, according to the power that worketh in us.” (Ephesians 3:20)

“A wise man will hear and will increase learning; and a man of understanding shall attain unto wise counsels.” (Proverbs 1:5)

“Knowing this, that the trying of your faith worketh patience. But let patience have her perfect work, that ye may be perfect and entire, wanting nothing.” (James 1: 3-4)

Prayer Point:

Father God, I pray your word as in Matthew 7:7 that I shall Ask, and it shall be given until me. For you have blessed me with spiritual blessings in heavenly places in Christ Jesus. Father, at this moment, I ask for an increase in wisdom for you giveth to all men liberally to include an increase in understanding for your word says I shall not lean to my own understanding but put my faith and trust in you. In Jesus’ mighty name, I pray. Amen.

DEALING WITH ANGER AND WRATH

After experiencing strife and offense, the enemy's tactic is to cause you to lose people in your life by developing uncontrollable feelings of anger and hate towards them, thereby introducing wrath.

Scriptures:

"A quick-tempered person does foolish things, and the one who devises evil schemes is hated." (Proverbs 14:17 NIV)

"Sensible people control their temper; they earn respect by overlooking wrongs." (Proverbs 19:11)

"A man without self-control is like a city broken into and left without walls." (Proverbs 25:28)

"Whoso keepeth his mouth and his tongue keepeth his soul from troubles." (Proverbs 21:23)

"Death and life are in the power of the tongue: and they that love it shall eat the fruit thereof." (Proverbs 18:21)

Prayer Point:

Father God, I pray that the Holy Spirit will remind me that death and life are in the power of the tongue. Father, I pray to not be like a city broken into and left without walls. I pray to be sensible as in Proverbs 19:11 for whoso keepeth his mouth and his tongue keepeth his soul from trouble and yields patience. In Jesus' name, I pray. Amen.

Actionable Steps:

When you are about to have a conversation with someone that usually turns into a disagreement or argument, then you need to pray before talking to that person. Pray a prayer like the one above. Ask the LORD to bridle your tongue. Remind yourself to let them talk, try not to respond too quickly. Choose your battles wisely. Is a discussion with them worth disrupting your peace? Will stating your opinion change anything? Are you communicating with a reasonable person or a fool? The Bible says, “Answer not a fool according to his folly, lest thou also be like unto him” (Proverbs 26:4).

REPEATING PAST – SPIRIT OF BACKWARDNESS & DELAY

If you are continuing to have the same problems, getting involved in toxic relationships (same person, different name), and you always seem to miss great opportunities, the enemy may be sowing the spirit of backwardness and delay while you sleep. These spirits hinder your progress in life and prevent you from moving forward.

Below is an example of a prayer you should declare over your life. Do not have any doubt as you say this prayer. Remember, John 10:10 says, "The thief cometh not, but for to steal, and to kill, and to destroy: I am come that they might have life, and that they might have it more abundantly."

Prayer Point:

Father God, I pray over every evil power and chain of witchcraft that is being used to create failure, backwardness, and delay, I declare John 10:10. For you said he came to give me life and more abundantly. For the LORD is my rock, my fortress, and my deliverer from the snares of the enemy. For according to his word in Jeremiah 23:29, his word is like a fire, a hammer that breaketh the rock in pieces and the righteous shall be recompensed in the earth: much more the wicked and the sinner. This I declare in the name of my LORD and Savior Jesus Christ, Amen.

Actionable Steps:

Stop immediately dating the same type of people and heal yourself first. Do not date people based on superficial things like money and looks. Journal about what you find appealing in these people and why you desire to be with them. Do you have a spirit of rejection? Were you abused, rejected, or neglected when you were younger? Did you recover from that trauma? Have you forgiven those who hurt you? Do you need to work on your self-esteem? See Chapter 12. Look at the areas in your life where you are experiencing delay and backwardness. If it's financial, start being a blessing to someone who cannot promote you or do anything physically for you. See chapter 24 for examples.

YOUR CHILDREN'S BEHAVIOR IS UNREAL

When you speak negative words concerning your children, you are cursing them. For example, when you are cursing their father, spiritually, you are cursing your children and yourself. When you complain about their behavior, you cause their behavior to increase. You are fueling the spirit realm to show that you agree by complaining and declaring that your children are stupid, liars, thieves, whoremongers, or will never amount to anything.

If your children's behavior seems extreme, then look at their entertainment. Check to see if they are getting exposed to satanic programming by looking at the music videos, cartoons, movies, toys, video games, and social media they enjoy. Listen to how they talk to their friends when they think no one is listening. Do they have self-esteem issues? Do they follow along with everything their friends say? Does your children have suicidal thoughts, cut themselves, have angry outbursts, or use lots of profanity? Do they steal, are obsessed with their looks, or being liked by others? Do they constantly cry or want to stay to themselves?

These are questions you need to ask yourself before going straight into punishment mode as well as are they exhibiting signs of abuse whether physically or sexually? Are there certain adults or older teenagers they do not want to come to the house or be left alone with? If you know of the abuse but haven't done anything about it out of fear, shame, or disgrace, then you are a contributor to their abuse.

Actionable Steps:

If your children has demonic toys, games, and other

paraphernalia, you need to have a discussion with your children regarding the effects of these items and suggest getting rid of them. If you have a teenager, do not go on a rampage and just get rid of everything. Start with one thing at a time. For instance, "I notice you been a little short tempered lately, and I think it's due to the violence on the video games. I want you to give up video games for 2 weeks so I can see if this changes your behavior. If so, you can have them back."

In the meantime, if you are a righteous parent or guardian. Start praying, "Father God, I bind and rebuke the spirit of anger and rage in my child. I declare your word as in Proverbs 11:21 that the seed of the righteous shall be delivered". Father, remove the desire from my child to play video games and replace it with a desire to know you. In Jesus' mighty name I pray, Amen."

Next, if you feel your child has self-esteem issues due to withdrawing from others or being rebellious, think about whether your child developed a spirit of rejection in the womb because he or she was an unwanted pregnancy. Did you ever say you wished they were never born? Do you favor or constantly brag about other children? Do you show them love in the way he or she likes to receive it? Don't let your personal feeling of rejection prevent you from discipline your children for undiscipline children will bring shame onto you. Seek to find the root cause for the behavior before taking action. See chapter 12 for more information regarding feelings, emotions, and thoughts.

Scriptures:

"My people are destroyed for lack of knowledge: because thou hast rejected knowledge, I will also reject thee, that thou shalt be no priest to me: seeing thou hast forgotten the law of thy God, I will also forget thy children." (Hosea 4:6)

"Praise ye the LORD. Blessed is the man that feareth the LORD, that delighteth greatly in his commandments. His seed shall be mighty upon earth: the generation of the upright shall be blessed." (Psalm 112:1-2)

"Train up a child in the way he should go and when he is old, he will not depart from it." (Proverbs 22:6)

"Though hand join in hand, the wicked shall not be unpunished: but the seed of the righteous shall be delivered." (Proverbs 11:21)

"When Jesus saw that the people came running together, he rebuked the foul spirit, saying unto him, thou dumb and deaf spirit, I charge thee, come out of him, and enter no more into him." (Mark 9:25)

Prayer Point:

Father God, I declare your word that my seed shall be delivered as in Proverbs 11:21. For I train my child up in your word and let it not depart from him. For my desire is only good and the name of the LORD is a strong tower; and I run to it asking for deliverance for my child from the spirt of __________, __________, __________. As it is written, the LORD will bless the righteous and surround me with a shield of love. For since I find you, I find life and shall obtain favor of the LORD. In Jesus' mighty name, I pray. Amen.

(replace the underline with the applicable sin)

Note: Stop saying your child has ADHD or ADD! Remember the power of the tongue in Proverbs 18:21 instead declare your child has a sound mind as in 2 Timothy 1:7 and self-control like in 2 Peter 1:6 or Galatians 5:22.

BITTERNESS IS YOUR RIGHT?

Disappointment leads to feelings of betrayal and distrust. This bitterness can allow negative influences to take root, potentially leading to harmful behaviors, such as seeking revenge or engaging in witchcraft. Additionally, the anger that you feel is a form of jealousy directed towards God, since you feel life is unfair and reject the notion of enduring suffering.

Scriptures:

"Let all bitterness, and wrath, and anger, and clamour, and evil speaking, be put away from you, with all malice. And be ye kind one to another, tenderhearted, forgiving one another, even as God for Christ's sake hath forgiven you." (Ephesians 4:31-32)

"The Spirit lifted me up and took me away. I went into bitterness and turmoil, but the LORD's hold on me was strong." (Ezekiel 3:14 NLT)

"Looking diligently lest any man fail of the grace of God; lest any root of bitterness springing up trouble you, and thereby many be defiled." (Hebrews 12:15)

Prayer Point:

Father God, I ask for repentance of my sins for allowing bitterness to take root. For your word said I will be defiled if I let bitterness sink in. Therefore, I am declaring for all bitterness, wrath, and anger to be put away from me. For I am agreeing with your word in Ephesians 4:32, to forgive one another as God for Christ's sake has forgiven me. In Jesus' mighty name, I pray. Amen.

Actionable Steps:

Keep a gratitude journal and make a point to write in it every day. Recognize the blessings that you have. Do all your senses work? Can you get dressed without any assistance? Have you ever gone without food unintentionally? Do you have loving parents, grandparents, children, spouse, partner, or friends? Are you able to travel? Have you completed your degree? Next, when you feel betrayed, remember Judas betrayed Jesus, so if the King of Kings can get betrayed, then how likely are you to get betrayed too? Last, remember you want forgiveness, so don't speak any evil regarding them, and remember God sees everything. Just be mindful when you must deal with certain people and keep your personal business to yourself.

DEALING WITH CONFLICT WITH EXPERTISE

Pray for your enemies because your anointing will start working against them. Don't pray curses against them, but rebuke and bind the spirit of hate, envy, jealousy, lying, slander, and deception operating in them.

Scriptures:

"And we know that all things work together for good to them that love God, to them who are the called according to his purpose." (Romans 8:28)

"Let all bitterness, and wrath, and anger, and clamour, and evil speaking, be put away from you, with all malice: And be ye kind one to another, tenderhearted, forgiving one another, even as God for Christ's sake hath forgiven you." (Ephesians 4:31-32)

"When a man's ways please the LORD, he maketh even his enemies to be at peace with him." (Proverbs 16:7)

"A soft answer turneth away wrath: but grievous words stir up anger." (Proverbs 15:1)

"Whoso keepeth his mouth and his tongue keepeth his soul from troubles." (Proverbs 21:23)

"A fool uttereth all his mind: but a wise man keepeth it in till afterwards." (Proverbs 29:11)

"No weapon formed against you shall prosper, and every tongue which rises against you in judgment You shall condemn. This is the heritage of the servants of the LORD, and their righteousness is from Me," says the LORD." (Isaiah 54:17)

“Death and life are in the power of the tongue, and those who love it will eat its fruit.” (Proverbs 18:21)

“Rejoice not when thine enemy falleth and let not thine heart be glad when he stumbleth: Lest the LORD see it, and it displease him, and he turn away his wrath from him.” (Proverbs 24:17)

“For I know the thoughts that I think toward you, says the LORD, thoughts of peace and not of evil, to give you a future and a hope.” (Jeremiah 29:11)

“For we wrestle not against flesh and blood, but against principalities, against powers, against the rulers of the darkness of this world, against spiritual wickedness in high places.” (Ephesians 6:12)

“He that is slow to anger is better than the mighty; and he that ruleth his spirit than he that taketh a city.” (Proverbs 16:32)

“The discretion of a man deferreth his anger; and it is his glory to pass over a transgression.” (Proverbs 19:11)

“He that hath no rule over his own spirit is like a city that is broken down, and without walls.” (Proverbs 25:28)

“Wherefore, my beloved brethren, let every man be swift to hear, slow to speak, slow to wrath: For the wrath of man worketh not the righteousness of God.” (James 1:19 – 20)

“‘A man's foes shall be they of his own household.’ Those that are close to you are the ones the enemy uses to get to you.” (Matthew 10:36)

‘He that keepeth his mouth keepeth his life: but he that openeth wide his lips shall have destruction.” (Proverbs 13:3)

“Answer not a fool according to his folly, lest thou also be like unto him.” (Proverbs 26:4)

“Go from the presence of a foolish man, when thou perceivest not in him the lips of knowledge.” (Proverbs 14:7)

"I said, I will take heed to my ways, that I sin not with my tongue: I will keep my mouth with a bridle, while the wicked is before me." (Psalm 39:1)

"Whoso keepeth his mouth and his tongue keepeth his soul from troubles." (Proverbs 21:23)

"Dearly beloved, avenge not yourselves, but rather give place unto wrath: for it is written, Vengeance is mine; I will repay, saith the Lord." (Romans12:19)

Prayer Point:

Father, I pray to be loose from anger, bitterness, and revenge. I declare according to your word in 2 Corinthians 10:5, that I must cast down imaginations, and bring every thought to the obedience of Christ. I pray to keep my mouth with a bridle as your words says in Psalm 39:1 when dealing with the wicked. For I shall be swift to hear, slow to speak, slow to wrath, for all things work together for my good in Jesus mighty name, I pray. Amen.

CHALLENGES WITH YOUR MIND:

Feelings, Emotions, Thoughts

Enemy Operating in the Mind

Abandonment Bitterness Confusion Depression
Despair Disappointment Discouragement Doubt
Forgetfulness Heaviness Indecision Insanity
Loneliness Misery Offense Rejection Schizophrenia
Self-Destruction Self-Pity Slumber Suicidal
Tiredness Torment Unbelief UnforgivenesS

Remember each spirit objective is to open the door for other spirits to gain entry. For example, the spirit of discouragement, rejection, and offense are shown below.

Discouragement – Depression – Oppression – Suicide
Rejection – Anger – Control – Rebellion
Offense–Disappointment–Resentment
Unforgiveness-Bitterness-Witchcraft

Scriptures:

"Wisdom is the principal thing; therefore get wisdom: and with all thy getting get understanding." (Proverbs 4:7)

“For the LORD giveth wisdom: out of his mouth cometh knowledge and understanding. He layeth up sound wisdom for the righteous: he is a buckler to them that walk uprightly.” (Proverbs 2:6-7)

"But the wisdom that is from above is first pure, then peaceable, gentle, and easy to be intreated, full of mercy and good fruits, without partiality, and without
hypocrisy." (James 3:17)

“Who is a wise man and endued with knowledge among you? let him shew out of a good conversation his works with meekness of wisdom." (James 3:13)

"Casting down imaginations, and every high thing that exalteth itself against the knowledge of God and bringing into captivity every thought to the obedience of Christ." (2 Corinthians 10:5)

"Trust in the LORD with all thine heart; and lean not unto thine own understanding. In all thy ways acknowledge him, and he shall direct thy paths." (Proverbs 3:5-6)

"A double minded man is unstable in all his ways." (James 1:8)

"For in many things we offend all. If any man offends not in word, the same is a perfect man, and able also to bridle the whole body." (James 3:2)

"And blessed is he, whosoever shall not be offended in me. When you get to the point that you continue to help those that offended you without criticism or negative talk. You have just elevated to the next level in God's kingdom." (Luke 7:23)

"Knowing this, that the trying of your faith worketh patience. But let patience have her perfect work, that ye may be perfect and entire, wanting nothing." (James 1: 3-4)

"To appoint unto them that mourn in Zion, to give unto them beauty for ashes, the oil of joy for mourning, the garment of praise for the spirit of heaviness; that they might be called trees of righteousness, the planting of the LORD, that he might be glorified." (Isaiah 61:3)

"Then Peter said unto them, Repent, and be baptized every one of you in the name of Jesus Christ for the remission of sins, and ye shall receive the gift of the Holy Ghost." (Acts 2:38)

"For God is not the author of confusion, but of peace, as in all churches of the saints." (1 Corinthians 14:33)

"My soul melteth for heaviness: Strengthen thou me according unto thy word." (Psalms 119:28)

"Casting all your care upon him; for he careth for you." (Peter 5:7)

"Blessed is the man that trusteth in the LORD, and whose hope the LORD is." (Jeremiah 17:7)

"Have not I commanded thee? Be strong and of a good courage; be not afraid, neither be thou dismayed: for the LORD thy God is with thee whithersoever thou goest." (Joshua 1:9)

"Cast thy burden upon the LORD, and he shall sustain thee: He shall never suffer the righteous to be moved." (Psalm 55:22)

"Let not your heart be troubled: ye believe in God, believe also in me." (John 14:1)

"Therefore I say unto you, Take no thought for your life, what ye shall eat, or what ye shall drink; nor yet for your body, what ye shall put on. Is not the life more than meat, and the body than raiment? Behold the fowls of the air: for they sow not, neither do they reap, nor gather into barns; yet your heavenly Father feedeth them. Are ye not much better than they? Which of you by taking thought can add one cubit unto his stature?" (Matthew 6:25-27)

"Say to them that are of a fearful heart, Be strong, fear not: behold, your God will come with vengeance, even God with a recompence; he will come and save you." (Isaiah 35:4)

"The righteous cry, and the LORD heareth, And delivereth them out of all their troubles." (Psalms 34:17)

"I will say of the LORD, He is my refuge and my fortress: My God; in him will I trust." (Psalms 91:2)

"Many there be which say of my soul, There is no help for him in God. Selah. But thou, O LORD, art a shield for me; My glory, and the lifter up of mine head. I cried unto the LORD with my voice, And he heard me out of his holy hill. Selah. I laid me down and slept; I awaked; for the LORD sustained me." (Psalms 3:2-5)

"The LORD also will be a refuge for the oppressed, A refuge in times of trouble. And they that know thy name will put their trust in thee: For thou, LORD, hast not forsaken them that seek thee." (Psalms 9:9)

"God is our refuge and strength, A very present help in trouble." (Psalms 46:1)

"My flesh and my heart faileth: But God is the strength of my heart, and my portion forever." (Psalms 73:26)

Prayer Point:

Father God, I bind the spirit of depression and anxiety with the same spirit that raised Christ from the dead, for the same spirit dwells in me, so therefore I bind and declare the blood of Jesus against you and command you to leave now. Father God, I pray for wisdom that is from above as in James 3:17 and to cast down imaginations and every high thing that exalteth itself against the knowledge of you. In Jesus' mighty name, I pray. Amen.

(REPLACE UNDERLINE WITH YOUR SIN)

Also, pray for God to help you in the areas where doubt and unbelief try to come upon you. Remember, God's word does not come back void.

Actionable Steps:

Avoid listening to sad/depressing movies or songs. Don't watch demonic, horror, or drama filled shows especially before going to sleep. Stop eating or drinking excessively, remind yourself to bring every negative thought to captivity, start pursuing activities like walking, exercising, gardening, painting, photography, reading, and watching cooking videos. Also, try to eliminate or reduce communication with toxic people.

Exercises:
Challenge the enemy by saying the opposite of the negative thought.

Enemy: I am ugly, and no one wants me
Challenge: Father God, your word says I am wonderfully made

Enemy: I am so stupid
Challenge: Father God, your word says the mind of the righteous is blessed

I highly recommend listening to Stephen Darby's message 'Recover from Schizophrenia" for a list of evil spirits that affect the mind.

ENVY AND JEALOUSY:

The Green-Eyed Monster

Jealousy - Envy - Discontentment - Anger

Rage - Violence - Coveting - Bitterness

Jealousy occurs when someone has an inferiority complex. Envy is the desire to have an item or an experience that someone else possesses. When there is envy and strife, there is confusion in the works. Jealousy comes in when you don't see what God has done for you.

Scriptures:

"Love is patient and kind. Love is not jealous, boastful, or proud." (1 Corinthians 13:4 NLT)

"Be not thou envious against evil men, neither desire to be with them." (Proverbs 24:1)

"Let us not be desirous of vain glory, provoking one another, envying one another." (Galatians 5:26)

"Fret not thyself because of evildoers, neither be thou envious against the workers of iniquity." (Psalm 37:1)

"Envy thou not the oppressor and choose none of his ways." (Proverbs 3:31)

Prayer Point:

Father God, I ask for forgiveness of my sins and to cleanse my heart of envy and jealousy. For I bind myself to your word that says love is patient and kind, and not jealous or proud. I thank you that you blessed me with favor and mercy all the days of my life along with blessing me with spiritual blessings in heavenly places according to Ephesians 1:3. Father God, I rebuke the spirit of comparison and take pleasure in serving you. In Jesus' mighty name I pray. Amen.

Actionable Steps:

Some of the most well-dressed people have low self-esteem in which they dress up to hide their disfunction. If you suffer from depression and have low self-esteem issues, try to limit your social media usage. Be mindful of how you feel when you see certain postings, either snooze or unfollow them. Do not post anything unless it's necessary for your business, for you will continuously be checking to see how many likes you get or if a particular person watched a video or liked your picture. You will post more and more to get more gratification and fulfillment, but the moment the number of likes decreases, your videos are not being watch, or the person that you wanted to see your posting either stops looking or blocks you, then depression and more self-esteem issues will sink in. You will stop posting for fun and post for confirmation that you are worthy. You will crave the attention like a drug, and the enemy will use this to his advantage to get you even more in a depressing state.

Other questions to ask yourself: Why you are feeling jealous regarding this person or group? Is it because they have something you have been wanting? Are they extremely attractive and you wish you looked like them? Do you envy their talents or skills? Do you feel neglected, unseen, unloved? Are they living the life that you desire? If any of these things are true, then write down how you really feel and start taking actionable steps to get rid of that feeling. Realize that no one has it all and keep a journal of all the things you are grateful for. Also, thank God for those blessings you currently have. Remember, comparison obstructs your peace, so focus on what brings you joy. Fill those moments that you are usually on Facebook and Instagram with a hobby, spending time with family or friends, or simply relaxing and enjoying peace and quiet.

ENEMIES AND THEIR EVIL ALTARS

Altars are used to summon and submit sacrifices to either Jehovah (the Most High) or evil spirits.

Pastor Kevin LA Ewing's favorite verse is Hosea 4:6, "My people are destroyed for lack of knowledge." This is so true after I realize that most things that happen to us were first established in the spiritual realm.

"But while men slept, his enemy came and sowed tares among the wheat and went his way." (Matthew 13:25)

Demons with the help of witches, warlocks, sorcerers, and wizards use your dreams to establish covenants and bring curses to you. Most of these satanists uses items such as your clothing, hair, fingernails, personal items, and pictures to send curses (evil spirits) into your life. Some signs there could be an evil altar erected against you are extreme feelings of sadness and depression, suicidal thoughts, constant nightmares, eating in a dream, seeing water creatures, talking to the dead, sexual dreams, unexplained sickness, relationship issues, confusion, infirmities, forgetfulness, and laziness.

They use witchcraft to manipulate, torment, and destroy you. Evil spirits, witches and warlocks monitor your behavior, what you say, and what your weaknesses are to plot against you. The devil sets up schemes, plots, hinderances, delays, and limitations to keep you from fulfilling your purpose. These spiritual robbers are preventing you from reaching your full potential.

It may be stopping you from buying a house, getting promoted, getting married, starting a business, writing a book, etc. Today, social media is being heavily used by satanists to form connections with Christians.

Fasting is the key to gaining victory in this world. When you buffet your body, you can hear from God more clearly. Isaiah 58:6 states, "Is this not the fast that I have chosen: To loose the bonds of wickedness, to undo the heavy burdens, to let the oppressed go free, and that you break every yoke? Fasting is so important that not only Christians but Satanists fast as well. The only difference is a true Christian has more power in the spiritual realm.

Books such as Jonah 3, Esther 4, and Ezra 8 shows examples of how fasting is used when facing a major problem. Every fasting scenario in the Bible required abstaining from food. Don't let the Pharisees deceived you in thinking you can fast in other ways!

Note: It is recommend to abstain from sex, even if you are married, but make sure you discuss this with your spouse before you start your fast.

After you fast, the demons will try to reinstate themselves via dreams, and this is when you need to renounce, rebuke, denounce, and reject those dreams. If you are signing something, eating or drinking, having sex, given money or gifts, breast feeding, getting married, receiving tattoos in your dreams, the enemy is trying to reestablish covenants and agreements.

When you are praying against evil altars, you have to be bold with your prayers. Just like how David was fearless with Goliath, the only way the enemy would take you seriously is to declare God's work and apply the name and blood of Jesus Christ. As a reminder, you are not praying against the warlock and witches at these evil altars. Instead, you are praying against the evil spirits. God says revenge is his according to Romans 12:19.

Start praying before you go to sleep and include Ephesians 6:13-18, and always say a prayer every morning to command your day after your renounce and rebuke all evil dreams, soul ties, covenants and agreements from Satan's kingdom.

Scriptures:

"Behold, I give unto you power to tread on serpents and scorpions, and over all the power of the enemy: and nothing shall by any means hurt you." (Luke 10:19)

"But ye shall destroy their altars, break their images, and cut down their groves." (Exodus 34:13)

"As the bird by wandering, as the swallow by flying, so the curse causeless shall not come." (Proverbs 26:2)

"For evildoers shall be cut off: but those that wait upon the Lord, they shall inherit the earth." (Psalm 37:9)

"While we look not at the things which are seen, but at the things which are not seen: for the things which are seen are temporal; but the things which are not seen are eternal." (2 Corinthians 4:18)

"The wicked flee when no man pursueth: but the righteous are bold as a lion." (Proverbs 28:1)

"And I will restore to you the years that the locust hath eaten, the cankerworm, and the caterpiller, and the palmerworm, my great army which I sent among you." (Joel 2:25)

"And I will cut off witchcrafts out of thine hand; and thou shalt have no more soothsayers." (Micah 5:12)

"The LORD shall cause thee to be smitten before thine enemies: thou shalt go out one way against them and flee seven ways before them: and shalt be removed into all the kingdoms of the earth." (Deuteronomy 28:7).

"When a man's ways please the LORD, he maketh even his enemies to be at peace with him." (Proverbs 16:7)

"No weapon that is formed against thee shall prosper; and every tongue that shall rise against thee in judgment thou shalt condemn. This is the heritage of the servants of the LORD, and their righteousness is of me, saith the LORD." (Isaiah 54:17)

"Whoso diggeth a pit shall fall therein: and he that rolleth a stone, it will return upon him." (Proverbs 26:27)

"Every word of God is pure: he is a shield unto them that put their trust in him." (Proverbs 30:5)

"From henceforth let no man trouble me: for I bear in my body the marks of the LORD Jesus." (Galatians 6:17)

"And I will bless them that bless thee and curse him him that curseth thee: and in thee shall all families of the earth be blessed." (Genesis 12:3)

"Therefore, if thine enemy hunger, feed him; if he thirsts, give him drink: for in so doing thou shalt heap coals of fire on his head." (Romans 12:20)

"Ye shall not need to fight in this battle: set yourselves, stand ye still, and see the salvation of the LORD with you, O Judah and Jerusalem: fear not, nor be dismayed; tomorrow go out against them: for the LORD will be with you." (2 Chronicles 20:17)

"The LORD bringeth the counsel of the heathen to nought: he maketh the devices of the people of none effect." (Psalm 33:10)

"When thou liest down, thou shalt not be afraid: yea, thou shalt lie down, and thy sleep shall be sweet." (Proverbs 3:24)

"The angel of the LORD encampeth round about them that fear him, and delivereth them." (Psalm 34:7)

"Put on the whole armour of God, that ye may be able to stand against the wiles of the devil." (Ephesians 6:11)

"So shall my word be that goeth forth out of my mouth: it shall not return unto me void, but it shall accomplish that which I please, and it shall prosper in the thing whereto I sent it." (Isaiah 55:11)

"But to which of the angels said he at any time, sit on my right hand, until I make thine enemies thy footstool? Are they not all ministering spirits, sent forth to minister for them who shall be heirs of salvation?" (Hebrews 1:13-14)

"For we wrestle not against flesh and blood, but against principalities, against powers, against the rulers of the darkness of this world, against spiritual wickedness in high places." (Ephesians 6:12)

"For the weapons of our warfare are not carnal, but mighty through God to the pulling down of strong holds." (2 Corinthians 10:4)

"Ye shall not make any cuttings in your flesh for the dead, nor print any marks upon you: I am the LORD." (Leviticus 19:28)

"If the Son therefore shall make you free, ye shall be free indeed." (John 8:36)

"Nay, in all these things we are more than conquerors through him that loved us." (Romans 8:37)

"For ye are bought with a price: therefore, glorify God in your body, and in your spirit, which are God's." (1 Corinthians 6:20)

"Verily I say unto you, Whatsoever ye shall bind on earth shall be bound in heaven: and whatsoever ye shall loose on earth shall be loosed in heaven." (Matthew 18:18)

"But I say unto you, love your enemies, bless them that curse you, do good to them that hate you, and pray for them which despitefully use you, and persecute you." (Matthew 5:44)

"The LORD is my shepherd; I shall not want. He maketh me to lie down in green pastures: He leadeth me beside the still waters. He restoreth my soul: He leadeth me in the paths of righteousness for his name's sake. Yea, though I walk through the valley of the shadow of death, I will fear no evil: for thou art with me; Thy rod and thy staff they comfort me. Thou preparest a table before me in the presence of mine enemies: Thou anointest my head with oil; my cup runneth over. Surely goodness and mercy shall follow me all the days of my life: And I will dwell in the house of the LORD forever." (Psalms 23:1-6)

Note: You cannot seek revenge against your enemies as stated in Matthew 5:44. When the LORD says blessed them that means do not intentionally cause them harm. Sometimes it's hard to pray for someone who has wronged you, but you have to find something good to pray about on their behalf. For instance, I prayed for someone to conceive who has been trying for years. I did not like her at all but when she expressed her feelings about wanting to become a mother, I thought this is what I need to pray to God for because despite her attitude I thought she would be a really good mom. As always, when I pray unselfishly for someone, God answered my prayers. She conceived the same month that I prayed for her.

Prayer Point:

Father God, I declare that my body is the temple of the Holy Ghost, and I was bought with a price. I shall glorify God in my body, spirit, and mind. Father God, I pray that every monitoring spirit that has infiltrated my home are blinded in Jesus' name. Let all household witches in my life be exposed. Silence every evil voice speaking and render every evil altar fashioned against me powerless. Father, I cover my mind, body, soul, will, and emotions in the blood of Jesus, as well as my family, our possessions, careers, and finances with his precious blood. I declare Michael, God's chief angel will stand guard as he hearkened to the words of the

LORD. I declare I shall have sweet sleep according to your word in Proverbs 3:24. Through the authority of Jesus Christ, I bind every spirit of delay, hindrance, anti-progress, confusion, double mindedness, forgetfulness, disgrace, poverty, setback, limitations, and unforgiveness. For I declare the Son of the Most High, Jesus Christ has set me free, so I am free indeed. In Jesus' mighty name I pray, Amen.

Note: If you live a life of repentance and don't have any unconfessed sins, then, just like in Numbers 23:20, a curse cannot be brought upon those that have been blessed by the LORD.

*A list of different kinds of evil altars can be found in Pastor Uzor Ndekwu's book, *Overthrowing Evil Altars*.*

FEAR IS NOT YOUR PORTION

Fear opens the door for other spirits like poverty and sickness to come into your life.

"And fear not them which kill the body but are not able to kill the soul: but rather fear him which is able to destroy both soul and body in hell." (Matthew 10:28) This verse helped me eliminate fear of man. Realizing anything that happens to you is not without God's approval, (the good and bad), so why worry about trying to please men, when they don't have the power and neither does Satan.

Scriptures:

"So do not fear, for I am with you; do not be dismayed, for I am your God. I will strengthen you and help you; I will uphold you with my righteous right hand." (Isaiah 41:10 NIV)

"God is our refuge and strength, a very present help in trouble." (Psalm 46:1)

"The fear of the LORD is to hate evil: pride, and arrogancy, and the evil way, and the froward (gossiping) mouth, do I hate." (Proverbs 8:13)

"The fear of the LORD is the beginning of knowledge: but fools despise wisdom and instruction." (Proverbs 1:7)

"In the fear of the LORD is strong confidence: and his children shall have a place of refuge." (Proverbs 14:26)

"They do not fear bad news; they confidently trust the LORD to care for them." (Psalm 112:7 NLT)

"The fear of the LORD is the instruction of wisdom; and before honour is humility." (Proverbs 15:33)

"For God hath not given us the spirit of fear; but of power, and of love, and of a sound mind." (2 Timothy 1:7)

"That thou mightest fear the LORD thy God, to keep all his statutes and his commandments, which I command thee, thou, and thy son, and thy son's son, all the days of thy life; and that thy days may be prolonged." (Deuteronomy 6:2)

"What time I am afraid, I will trust in thee. In God I will praise his word, In God I have put my trust; I will not fear what flesh can do unto me." (Psalms 56:3)

"Yea, though I walk through the valley of the shadow of death, I will fear no evil: for thou art with me; Thy rod and thy staff they comfort me." (Psalms 23:4)

"And the LORD, he it is that doth go before thee; he will be with thee, he will not fail thee, neither forsake thee: fear not, neither be dismayed." (Deuteronomy 31:8)

"I sought the LORD, and he heard me, And delivered me from all my fears." (Psalms 34:4)

Prayer Point:

Every time you start feeling anxious or fearful. Say to yourself or out loud.

Spirit of fear, I command you to leave right now. For I cover my place with the blood of Jesus; I outfit myself with the whole armor of God. My waist is girdled with truth, having on my breastplate of righteous, my feet shod with the preparation of the gospel of peace, my helmet of salvation, and the sword of the Spirit (God's Word), along with my shield of faith to quench all the fiery darts of the wicked. In Jesus' name I pray, Amen.

Or:

Spirit of fear, God didn't give a spirit of fear but of power, and of love, and of a sound mind and I declare his word over you. Therefore, I take authority over you with the blood of Jesus Christ, and I bind your demonic powers, and I command you by the shed blood of Jesus Christ to leave my life and my property in the name of Jesus Christ, my LORD and Savior. Amen.

Actionable Steps:

Avoid watching horror, drama filled movies, or depressing news channels. Don't look at sites or videos that stir fear to include avoid doom and gloom conversations.

GOSSIPING YOUR WAY TO DARKNESS

Blasphemy Criticism Cursing Exaggeration Gossip Lying Negative Talk Profanity Slander Swearing

When it comes to gossip, the world says that it is okay to share some tea, but is it really? Does it benefit your life or give the enemy access to you?

Scriptures:

"Wherefore laying aside all malice, and all guile, and hypocrisies, and envies, and all evil speakings." (1 Peter 2)

"He that keepeth his mouth keepeth his life: but he that openeth wide his lips shall have destruction." (Proverbs 13:3)

"An ungodly man digs up evil, and it is on his lips like a burning fire." (Proverbs 16:27)

"He that hideth hatred with lying lips, and he that uttereth a slander, is a fool." (Proverbs 10:18)

Actionable Steps:

Don't allow people to come to you with messages regarding slander/gossip. Guard your heart and your tongue, for this could lead to destruction. Some people just love to see drama and try to get you out of your peace. Stay off websites full of slander and gossip; they're being used to poison the spirit. Ask the LORD to bridle your tongue when you're around or talking to someone who pulls you into gossip. Try to remain quiet or do not chime into conversations full of gossip. Stand your ground by not offering an opinion and/or remaining neutral.

GREEDY AND NEVER SATISFIED

"No man can serve two masters: for either he will hate the one and love the other; or else he will hold to the one and despise the other. Ye cannot serve God and mammon." (Matthew 6:24)

The mammon spirit is the source of envy, greed, and lust to gain power and wealth over others. A person bound by this spirit cannot be trusted. Some will go into sex trafficking, pornography, blackmail, murder, bribery, even making a covenant with the devil to gain more wealth and power.

It's worth mentioning that 3 books in the Holy Bible state, "For what is a man profited, if he shall gain the whole world, and lose his own soul?" This means that it is extremely important that you don't follow this broad path down to get wealth because you will lose big time at the end.

Scriptures:

"For the love of money is the root of all evil: which while some coveted after, they have erred from the faith and pierced themselves through with many sorrows." (1 Timothy 6:10)

"So are the ways of everyone that is greedy of gain, which taketh away the life of the owners thereof." (Proverbs 1:19)

"He that is greedy of gain troubleth his own house; but he that hateth gifts shall live." (Proverbs 15:27)

"In thee have they taken gifts to shed blood; thou hast taken usury and increase, and thou hast greedily gained of thy neighbours by extortion, and hast forgotten me, saith the LORD God." (Ezekiel 22:12)

"Love not the world, neither the things that are in the world. If any man loves the world, the love of the Father is not in him." (1 John 2:15)

"He that loveth silver shall not be satisfied with silver; nor he that loveth abundance with increase: this is also vanity." (Ecclesiastes 5:10)

"Charge them that are rich in this world, that they be not highminded, nor trust in uncertain riches, but in the living God, who giveth us richly all things to enjoy." (1 Timothy 6:17)

"He that by usury and unjust gain increaseth his substance, he shall gather it for him that will pity the poor." (Proverbs 28:8)

Prayer Point:

Father God, I solemnly ask for forgiveness of my sins. I have let the spirit of mammon and greed consume me. I want to say I deeply apologize for all the hurt and pain I caused others. Father God, bless those I have wrongly used and manipulated out of their wealth. From this point forward, I want to abide in your commandments as in Deuteronomy 6:2 and conduct my business fairly, as in Psalm 112:5. For I will love not the world, neither the things that are in the world, but I choose to love you, the Father, the Most High, through Jesus Christ who strengthens me. In Jesus' mighty name, I pray. Amen.

Actionable Steps:

Cease all illegal or sinful activities to gain wealth and power. If you're a business owner, offer credit to those that you overcharged. Make it a point to earn money honestly and establish a new set of business rules to follow when conducting business. Ensure things like transparency and integrity are included in your business practices. In your personal life, do not date people because they have money. Take some time from dating to discover the real you, what qualities in a person you would like to have if money wasn't a factor. Focus on enjoying the simpler things in like and unsubscribe from social media influencers who will cause you to covet and lust after things. Instead look at other channels that inspire you to cook, garden, read, exercise, paint, etc. This will take your focus off money, but if you need help learning how to gain riches God's way, see chapter 24.

GRIEF: DON'T LET IT LEAD YOU TO NECROMANCY

When my brother passed away, I was out of town. He was 39 years old and experiencing heart problems. I suspected that he was going to die soon because I had a dream that someone was going to die a week before. Yet, I was determined to be strong and not let the enemy use that as an opportunity to bring in the spirit of grief and depression, although, there were moments when I saw everyone crying I started crying myself. I saw his lifeless body on the floor, and I reflected on the conversations that we had while he was in the hospital. He was scheduled to go to the heart doctor the next day since his appointment was rescheduled from the first week of the month to the last week of August 2024. Thoughts of anger and "what ifs" ran through our heads. Why did they reschedule him so far out when his heart was operating at 50 percent while experiencing blackouts? What if he had made his original appointment, would he still be with us? What if someone was in the house when he fainted? Could someone have called the ambulance in time to revive him? Did he know he was going to die soon? Did he get saved before he died? Did he really mean that he believed in God when he recited the sinner's prayer? All these questions arose while I, being the oldest, was still trying to be strong for everyone. I didn't want to talk about his death after his service nor did I announce the questions that I had concerning his death. I just wanted to acknowledge that God gave us a little more time with him and this place (earth) is not our permanent home. I praise God even more with gratitude that I had a brother, and I was able to connect more with him before he passed. I am thankful that I have a beautiful niece, his legacy. As a positive note, His passing away has made us tighter as a family. Phones calls to each other that used to normally go unanswered, are now being picked up or returned right away.

Shortly after his death, I had to remind my family that dreams concerning a loved one that passed are really masquerading demons appearing in their dreams to create a covenant with them. They try to get you to follow them, sign documents, or eat something in your dream. For those of you hearing this for the first time, you are not talking to your loved ones, you are forging covenants with demons (familiar spirits). Satan is using this opportunity to either bring sickness, infirmities, or poverty in your life. Note: Just because the dream seems harmless, that does not negate that you are dealing with demons. The enemy's mission is to kill, steal, and destroy!

If you take some time to think about your dream, you will notice the spirit is not an exact replica of your loved one, either in size, color, or facial features. Remember, the enemy can transform into an angel of light, per 2 Corinthians 11:14

Scriptures:

"To appoint unto them that mourn in Zion, to give unto them beauty for ashes, the oil of joy for mourning, the garment of praise for the spirit of heaviness; that they might be called trees of righteousness, the planting of the LORD, that he might be glorified." (Isaiah 61:3)

"The LORD is nigh unto them that are of a broken heart; and saveth such as be of a contrite spirit." (Psalm 34:18)

"For I reckon that the sufferings of this present time are not worthy to be compared with the glory which shall be revealed in us." (Romans 8:18)

"Fear thou not; for I am with thee be not dismayed; for I am thy God: I will strengthen thee; yea, I will help thee; yea, I will uphold thee with the right hand of my righteousness." (Isaiah 41:10)

"Blessed are they that mourn for they shall be

comforted." (Matthew 5:4)

“Blessed be God, even the Father of our LORD Jesus Christ, the Father of mercies, and the God of all comfort.” (2 Corinthians 1:3)

“And ye now therefore have sorrow: but I will see you again, and your heart shall rejoice, and your joy no man taketh from you.” (John 16:22)

“My soul melteth for heaviness: Strengthen thou me according unto thy word.” (Psalms 119:28)

“Surely he hath borne our griefs, and carried our sorrows: yet we did esteem him stricken, smitten of God, and afflicted. But he was wounded for our transgressions, he was bruised for our iniquities: the chastisement of our peace was upon him; and with his stripes we are healed.” (Isaiah 53:4-5)

“Come unto me, all ye that labour and are heavy laden, and I will give you rest. Take my yoke upon you, and learn of me; for I am meek and lowly in heart: and ye shall find rest unto your souls. For my yoke is easy, and my burden is light.” (Matthew 11:28-30)

For the living know that they shall die:
but the dead know not any thing,
neither have they any more a reward;
for the memory of them is forgotten.
Also their love, and their hatred, and their envy,
is now perished;
neither have they any more a portion
for ever in anything that is done under the sun.
Go thy way, eat thy bread with joy, and drink thy wine with a merry heart; for God now accepteth thy works. (Ecclesiastes 9: 5-7)
(Emphasis added)

Prayer Point:

Father God, I declare your word as in Matthew 5:4 to be comforted for the loss of my _______. I know you will strengthen me and help me for you are with me. For you are always near to those with a broken heart according to your word in Psalm 34:18, and therefore, Heavenly Father, I thank you for the oil of joy instead of mourning in Jesus' mighty name I pray. Amen.

Actionable Steps:

Always rebuke, renounce, and cancel any dreams of talking to the dead. Notice, I said dead (not loved ones). These are demons seeking a soul tie with you.

If what you need is to laugh and share the good times about your loved ones, connect with those that want to do the same. You may want to create a picture collage or keep some of their favorite things in a box for keepsake, but absolutely do not create a shrine. The goal is to be able to talk about them with joy and have peace in your heart when doing so. There is nothing wrong with crying over them after a certain time has passed but don't let the focus be on death. Instead, you are crying about the funny things they did or said that made you laugh. Start thanking God for blessing you to have them for a season. Remember this is not anyone's final destination.

Other positive ways to deal with grief are to look at videos of them often, embrace your pet or get a new pet, listen to their favorite music or watch a movie that they love, journal your thoughts/ emotions, in addition to seek grief counseling if needed. It doesn't matter how often you do this so long as you don't turn to drugs and alcohol. My mother watches videos of my brother as well as wears a shirt to family gatherings with a picture of him on it, and I in turn chose to write this book. These are just some of the ways my family has dealt with grief concerning the death of a parent, child, or sibling.

If memories of the person were unpleasant, then shift your praise to celebrate that you have passed the test, and that the relationship was used to strengthen you. It showed that you have what it takes to be on your own by pulling from your true source of strength, Jesus Christ.

INFIRMITIES & SICKNESS: STOP ACCEPTING THEM

Imagine if you pray God's word regarding sickness and infirmities over your life and you are healed without seeking a doctor. Have you noticed how a sickness or infirmity may skip someone in a family, or some family members continue to be cursed with a sickness or infirmity?

This could be because of a generational curse like the ones mentioned in Deuteronomy 7:15 or 2 Samuel 3:29; It can also be a result of an unconfessed and unrepentant lifestyle. I personally prayed Isaiah 53:5 during my 7-day fast. Two days during my fast, I woke up in excruciating pain, but I was determined not to take any medication because I was on a dry fast. I prayed that the LORD would remove the pain because I knew I was doing the right thing. I knew the Holy Spirit wanted me to complete the fast by telling me to not give up. So, I prayed that I didn't want to give up and I am healed through the stripes of Jesus Christ. Both times, I said the prayer, and I waited for God to stop the pain. The pain was gone in a matter of minutes.

Scriptures:

"That thou mightest fear the LORD thy God, to keep all his statutes and his commandments, which I command thee, thou, and thy son, and thy son's son, all the days of thy life; and that thy days may be prolonged." (Deuteronomy 6:2)

"But he was wounded for our transgressions, he was bruised for our iniquities: the chastisement of our peace was upon him; and with his stripes we are healed." (Isaiah 53:5)

“This fulfilled the word of the LORD through the prophet Isaiah, who said, ‘He took our sicknesses and removed our diseases.’” (Matthew 8:17)

“The LORD will strengthen him upon the bed of languishing: thou wilt make all his bed in his sickness.” (Psalm 41:3)

“He healeth the broken in heart, and bindeth up their wounds.” (Psalm 147:3)

“Heal me, O LORD, and I shall be healed; save me, and I shall be saved: for thou art my praise.” (Jeremiah 17:14)

”For I will restore health unto thee, and I will heal thee of thy wounds, saith the LORD; because they called thee an Outcast, saying, this is Zion, whom no man seeketh after.” (Jeremiah 30:17)

“And ye shall serve the LORD your God, and he shall bless thy bread, and thy water; and I will take sickness away from the midst of thee.” (Exodus 23:25)

“Bless the LORD, O my soul, and forget not all his benefits: Who forgiveth all thine iniquities; who healeth all thy diseases.” (Psalm 103:2-3)

“O LORD, by these things men live, and in all these things is the life of my spirit: so, wilt thou recover me, and make me to live.” (Isaiah 38:16)

“A merry heart doeth good like a medicine: but a broken spirit drieth the bones.” (Proverbs 17:22)

“Jesus said unto him, if thou canst believe, all things are possible to him that believeth.” (Mark 9:23)

“My son, attend to my words; incline thine ear unto my sayings. Let them not depart from thine eyes; keep them in the midst of thine heart. For they are life unto those that find them, and health to all their flesh.” (Proverbs 4:20-22).

“He sent his word, healed them, and delivered them from their destruction." (Psalm 107:20)

"He giveth power to the faint; and to them that have no might he increaseth strength". Even the youths shall faint and be weary, and the young men shall utterly fall: But they that wait upon the LORD shall renew their strength; they shall mount up with wings as eagles; they shall run, and not be weary; and they shall walk, and not faint." (Isaiah 40:29-31).

Prayer Point:

Father God, I repent for the sins on my mother's side and my father's side, I also ask for forgiveness of __________, ____________, ________________, and sins unknown. I am asking to be cleansed thoroughly by the blood of my LORD and Savior Jesus Christ. Father God, your word says all things are possible to him who believeth, and I am declaring that I am healed through the stripes of Jesus Christ and declaring Jeremiah 30:17 that says the LORD restores health unto me and heals me of my wounds. Therefore, every spirit of infirmity, sickness, accident, suicide, or death is bound by the blood of Jesus Christ. In Jesus' mighty name I pray, Amen.

(REPLACE UNDERLINE WITH YOUR SINS)

JEZEBEL IS BACK ON THE PROWL

Feminism is the religion of Jezebel where the wife is the head of the household and ruling over their effeminate husband and children. Those with a Jezebel spirit seek to marry people in authority so they can secretly pull the strings.

“Notwithstanding I have a few things against thee, because thou sufferest that woman Jezebel, which calleth herself a prophetess, to teach and to seduce my servants to commit fornication, and to eat things sacrificed unto idols.” (Revelation 2:20)

A Jezebel spirit is not limited to a female. Both sexes play the victim to get people to help them operate in the spirit. Using manipulation to gain control while behind the scenes shooting daggers behind your back. These people have a holy appearance and are usually very active in the church, but behind the scenes would tell lies, gossip, and cause strife amongst members to gain power and influence.

“People may cover their hatred with pleasant words, but they’re deceiving you. They pretend to be kind, but don’t believe them. Their hearts are full of many evils.” (Proverbs 26:24-25 NLT)

Another thing concerning the Jezebel spirit is that it attracts the Octopus spirit, which is a mind binding spirit. One of the symptoms of this spirit is experiencing severe migraines.

Prayer Point:

Father God, in the name of Jesus, I ask for forgiveness and deliverance from the Jezebel spirit. I repent for using manipulation and lies to get the things I want. I rebuke the Jezebel spirit and the Octopus spirit with all its tentacles. I demolish their strongholds in my mind and over my body. I command them to come out now. For the meek shall inherit the earth; and I shall be delighted in the abundance of peace. In Jesus' name I pray. Amen.

SEX, LUST, AND EVERYTHING ELSE YOU DESIRE

Perverted Desires and Appetites

Adultery Bestiality Fornication Homosexuality Incest Lesbianism Lust Masturbation Molestation Pedophilia Pornography Promiscuity Prostitution Rape Sexual Immorality Sexual Perversion Whoredom

Lust is a selfish uncontrollable passion or longing desire. Satan's goal is to tap into our natural drive and replaced that with lust; thereby getting us to abort our purpose.

When you sense that you are in a situation that may lead to lust, you need to leave the area as soon as possible. Repeat to yourself that you rebuke the spirit of lust, fornication, and adultery. According to Matthew 5:28, if you lust in your heart, it's considered adultery.

Evil spirits can transfer, so be careful of who you let lay hands on you. An example of this could be if you were molested, raped, or sexually assaulted, that spirit can transfer to you, especially if you are descendants to parents already living in habitual sin. This is the case when some people feel like they were born gay.

For those of you who feel this way, a question to ask could be: were you violated by a person of the same sex? Did you watch same sex porn? Some heterosexuals start developing homosexual desires for watching two women in porn but, in fact, Satan used those videos to create the desire to have sex with a man.

The same thing goes for a woman. Remember, the enemy is crafty! For example, anal sex is an example of witchcraft initiation. It's worship to Satan.

Scriptures:

"Lust not after her beauty in thine heart; neither let her take thee with her eyelids." (Proverbs 6:25)

"A man without self-control is like a city broken into and left without walls so build your walls with faith in God's word." (Proverbs 25:28)

"For this cause God gave them up unto vile affections: for even their women did change the natural use into that which is against nature: And likewise also the men, leaving the natural use of the woman, burned in their lust one toward another; men with men working that which is unseemly, and receiving in themselves that recompence of their error which was meet." (Romans 1:26 -27)

"But I say unto you, that whosoever looketh on a woman to lust after her hath committed adultery with her already in his heart." (Matthew 5:28)

Prayer Point:

Father God, I believe Jesus Christ died on the cross and, through him, I ask for forgiveness for committing ___________, _____________, ________________. I also ask for forgiveness for my sins unknown, for I am redeemed through his innocent blood. Father, I reject and bind the spirit of ___________, _____________, _____________. I bring them under the captivity of my LORD and Savior. I subdue them in the name of Jesus, I refuse to entertain these thoughts. I declare my body is a temple of the Holy Spirit and was bought for a price. Therefore, I shall always glorify God. Through his stripes I am delivered and dead to sin in accordance with 1 Peter 2:24, in Jesus' mighty name I pray and declare, Amen.

(REPLACE UNDERLINE WITH YOUR SIN)

Note: If your spouse is cheating on you, as a righteous spouse you have the authority to pray against what has your spouse bound. Take charge and pray against lust, adultery, fornication, and witchcraft.

Actionable Steps:

If you are trying to stop fornicating, don't continue to sleep on the mattress or bedding that you committed sin on. Avoid or fast forward through all sexual or kissing scenes on movies and shows. Absolutely, do not listen to sexually explicit songs or songs that you normally would play while having sex. Get rid of your sex toys, especially if you are a believer. This is still defilement. Try to cease all communication with your "circle of friends." You can't entertain sexual conversations or go to nightclubs anymore. You must get serious about taking steps to no longer be a victim. Every time you sleep with someone you are not married to, you are creating soul ties.

Note: There are so many implications for when you allow the temple of the Holy Spirt to be defiled.

MARINE KINGDOM AND UNWELCOME SPIRIT SPOUSE

Queen of India and Queen of Coasts are powerful water spirits. Within these kingdoms, hold seducing, unclean, water spirits from the marine kingdom. The most common evil spirits Incubus (spirit husbands) and Succubus or (Spirit Wives). Spirit spouses hinder marriages, cause barrenness, miscarriages, infirmities, and/or financial hardship.

If you have any sexual dreams, it's either an incubus, succubus, or a witch/warlock using a demon to astro-project to have sex with you to steal your virtue. Dreams of having kids or being pregnant, breast feeding, or carrying children in your arms as well as getting married or engaged are signs of these evil spirits. If you know of someone who has multiple spouses to die or experience several divorces. It's likely that they have a jealous spirit spouse that's causing those relationships to end. They also created thoughts of unfaithfulness, rage, unforgiveness, jealousy, and envy.

Spirit spouse have spiritual kids with their victims and thereby these demon kids cause miscarriages or women to become barren, for they do not want natural children to be born. If you suspect an incubus or succubus spirit, you must fast and pray. These are very stubborn spirits who try to capture you while you are sleeping. If you can, pray between midnight and 2 pm and try to disrupt their activity.

Not only do you sever ties with these evil spirits but with all the people you have slept with prior to getting married. If you were molested or raped, you must renounce and break the soul ties even though you were the victim. The spiritual realm operates completely different from the physical or natural realm. You must follow its rules to receive victory.

Scriptures:

"Howbeit this kind goeth not out but by prayer and fasting." (Matthew 17:21)

"Behold, I give unto you power to tread on serpents and scorpions, and over all the power of the enemy: and nothing shall by any means hurt you." (Luke 10:19)

"At thy rebuke they fled; at the voice of thy thunder, they hasted away." (Psalm 104:7)

"Out of the depths have I cried unto thee, O LORD." (Psalm 130)

"Cast forth lightning, and scatter them: shoot out thine arrows, and destroy them. Send thine hand from above; rid me, and deliver me out of great waters, from the hand of strange children." (Psalm 144:6-7)

"Yea, he sent out his arrows, and scattered them; and he shot out lightning, and discomfited them. Then the channels of water were seen, and the foundations of the world were discovered at thy rebuke, O LORD, at the blast of the breath of thy nostrils. He sent from above, he took me, he drew me out of many waters. He delivered me from my strong enemy, and from them which hated me: for they were too strong for me." (Psalm 18:14 -17)

"The voice of the LORD is upon the waters: the God of glory thundereth: the LORD is upon many waters." (Psalm 29:3)

"Dead things are formed from under the water, and the inhabitants thereof." (Job 26:5)

"Know ye not that ye are the temple of God, and that the Spirit of God dwelleth in you?" (1 Corinthians 3:16)

"The floods have lifted up, O LORD, the floods have lifted up their voice; the floods lift up their waves. The LORD on high is mightier than the noise of many waters, yea, than the mighty waves of the sea." (Psalm 93:3-4)

"Verily I say unto you, Whatsoever ye shall bind on earth shall be bound in heaven: and whatsoever ye shall loose on earth shall be loosed in heaven." (Matthew 18:18)

"But now thus saith the LORD that created thee, O Jacob, and he that formed thee, O Israel, Fear not: for I have redeemed thee, I have called thee by thy name; thou art mine. When thou passest through the waters, I will be with thee; and through the rivers, they shall not overflow thee: when thou walkest through the fire, thou shalt not be burned; neither shall the flame kindle upon thee." (Isaiah 43:1-2)

Prayer Points:

Father God, I severed every covenant with the marine kingdom and command these spirits to come out, now. For I break every evil marriage in the spirit realm, for my covenant is with Jesus. I declare you evil waters are saturated with the blood of Jesus Christ. For the LORD sent thine hand from above; rid me and deliver me out of great waters as in Psalm 144:7. The voice of the LORD is upon the waters: the God of glory thundereth: At thy rebuke you flee; at the voice of thy thunder you hast away. I declare every spirit of pride, witchcraft, and mind binding spirit received holy fire as I release the sword of the LORD against you and every spirit from the marine kingdom for my God has given me the authority to tread on serpents and scorpions, and over all the power of the enemy: and nothing shall by any means hurt me. In Jesus' name, I declare. Amen.

Other Water Spirits and their Characteristics

Leviathan-prideful, self-righteousness, stubbornness, confusion, chaos

Python-weariness, overwhelm, hopelessness, helpless, divination, witchcraft

Rahab-strife, discord, haughtiness

Squid and Octopus-mind binding spirits that create mental illness, depression, bipolar, anxiety, insanity, schizophrenia

Note: Other dreams regarding water spirits include dreaming of fish, crocodiles, alligators, octopus, large bodies of water. You can find more information regarding water spirits by reading “The Spiritual Warrior’s Guide to Defeating Water Spirits” by Jennifer Leclaire.

PERFECT PEACE IS YOURS

Over time in my spiritual journey, I started to experience peace. I was still going through a lot of spiritual warfare, still single but not lonely, and started realizing that a lot of people who I thought were my friends were merely associates (You will find out who really are your friends when you need them).

Despite all the challenges and trials over the years, I have developed perfect peace in knowing that when the time comes for judgement, I will be in the 3rd heaven with my God and my LORD Jesus Christ. Although I sin every day, I don't feel any condemnation (Romans 8:1) because the LORD sees my heart and I have a relationship with him through fasting and prayer, for he definitely knows my name!

Scriptures:

"Peace, I leave with you; my peace I give you. I do not give to you as the world gives. Do not let your heart be troubled and do not be afraid." (John 14:27 NIV)

"Thou wilt keep him in perfect peace, whose mind is stayed on thee: because he trusteth in thee." (Isaiah 26:3)

"Great peace have they which love thy law: and nothing shall offend them." (Psalm 119:165)

"My son, forget not my law; but let thine heart keep my commandments: For length of days, and long life, and peace, shall they add to thee." (Proverbs 3:1-2)

"For I know the thoughts that I think toward you, saith the LORD, thoughts of peace, and not of evil, to give you an expected end." (Jeremiah 29:11)

"And let the peace of God rule in your hearts, to the which also ye are called in one body; and be ye thankful." (Colossians 3:15)

"For unto us a child is born, unto us a son is given, and the government shall be upon his shoulder: and his name shall be called Wonderful, Counsellor, The mighty God, The everlasting Father, The Prince of Peace." (Isaiah 9:6)

"Now the Lord of peace himself give you peace always by all means. The Lord be with you all." (2 Thessalonians 3:16)

Prayer Point:

Father God, according to your word in Isaiah 26. You will keep me in perfect peace for I trust in you and my thoughts are fixed upon you as my eternal rock. I declare your word as in Colossians 3:15 to let the peace of God rule my heart. In Jesus' mighty name, I pray. Amen.

Follow up:

Thank God for the peace and favor upon your life and know he has already answered your prayer. He was just waiting on you to petition him.

Actionable Steps:

Read the Bible more, listen to sermons on YouTube, recognize that no storm last forever, don't concern yourself about things that are not under your control. Repeat that you will not be given more than you can handle. Rebuke the spirit of worry and anxiety, remember that no matter what, God loves you. Talk to God more often. Get out of toxic relationships. Focus on good things that make you happy. Get control of your finances. Declare God's word (blessings) over your life. Stop watching horror or movies involving lots of drama. Saty away from new age books and listening to music that makes you want to fight, get high, or have sex.

YOU NEED A FINANCIAL BLESSING

If you are experiencing financial hardship, job loss, spending beyond your means, or having a tough time finding employment, take note of the dreams that you've been having recently.

Are you seeing rats, roaches, spending excessive money, wearing worn-out clothing, losing money, or picking up coins in a dream? This represents the spirit of poverty. There are many other dreams that can represent poverty that are discussed on Pastor Kevin LA Ewing's blog or on his YouTube channel.

Immediately after having these dreams, you need to cancel, rebuke, and terminate them, or the enemy will have legal right because your silence is an agreement in the spirit realm.

Scriptures:

"And it shall be, when the LORD thy God shall have brought thee into the land which he sware unto thy fathers, to Abraham, to Isaac, and to Jacob, to give thee great and goodly cities, which thou buildedst not, And houses full of all good things, which thou filledst not, and wells digged, which thou diggedst not, vineyards and olive trees, which thou plantedst not; when thou shalt have eaten and be full." (Deuteronomy 6:10-11)

"They share freely and give generously to those in need. Their good deeds will be remembered forever." (Psalm 112:9 NLT)

"Good comes to those who lend money generously and conduct their business fairly. Such people will not be overcome by evil. Those who are righteous will be long remembered." (Psalm 112:5 NLT)

"And my God will meet all your needs according to the riches of his glory in Christ Jesus." (Philippians 4:19 NIV)

"Give, and it shall be given unto you; good measure, pressed down, and shaken together, and running over, shall men give into your bosom. For with the same measure that ye mete withal it shall be measured to you again." (Luke 6:38)

"Behold, the righteous shall be recompensed in the earth: much more the wicked and the sinner." (Proverbs 11:31)

"Then said he also to him that bade him, when thou makest a dinner or a supper, call not thy friends, nor thy brethren, neither thy kinsmen, nor thy rich neighbours; lest they also bid thee again, and a recompence be made thee. But when thou makest a feast, call the poor, the maimed, the lame, the blind: And thou shalt be blessed; for they cannot recompense thee: for thou shalt be recompensed at the resurrection of the just." (Luke 14:12-14)

"And I have given you a land for which ye did not labour, and cities which ye built not, and ye dwell in them; of the vineyards and oliveyards which ye planted not do ye eat." (Joshua 24:13)

"Give freely and become wealthier; be stingy and lose everything." (Proverbs 11:24 NLT)

"In that I command thee this day to love the LORD thy God, to walk in his ways, and to keep his commandments and his statutes and his judgments, that thou mayest live and multiply: and the LORD thy God shall bless thee in the land whither thou goest to possess it." (Deuteronomy 30:16)

"For the LORD God is a sun and shield: the LORD will give grace and glory: no good thing will he withhold from them that walk uprightly." (Psalm 84:11)

"Blessed is the man Who walks not in the counsel of the ungodly, nor stands in the path of sinners, nor sits in the seat of the scornful; But his delight is in the law of the LORD, And in His law, he meditates day and night. He shall be like a tree Planted by the rivers of water, That brings forth its fruit in its season, whose leaf also shall not wither; And whatever he does shall prosper."(Psalms 1:1–3)

“Wherefore it shall come to pass, if ye hearken to these judgments, and keep, and do them, that the LORD thy God shall keep unto thee the covenant and the mercy which he sware unto thy fathers: And he will love thee, and bless thee, and multiply thee: he will also bless the fruit of thy womb, and the fruit of thy land, thy corn, and thy wine, and thine oil, the increase of thy kine, and the flocks of thy sheep, in the land which he sware unto thy fathers to give thee. Thou shalt be blessed above all people: there shall not be male or female barren among you, or among your cattle.” (Deuteronomy 7:12-14)

“There is that scattereth, and yet increaseth; and there is that withholdeth more than is meet, but it tendeth to poverty. The liberal soul shall be made fat: and he that watereth shall be watered also himself.” (Proverbs 11:24-25 NKJ)

“But this I say, He which soweth sparingly shall reap also sparingly; and he which soweth bountifully shall reap also bountifully. Every man according as he purposeth in his heart, so let him give; not grudgingly, or of necessity: for God loveth a cheerful giver.” (2 Corinthians 9:6-7)

He that hath a bountiful eye shall be blessed; for he giveth of his bread to the poor. (Proverbs 22:9)

Prayer Point:

Father God, I pray your word that says you will meet all my needs according to the riches of your glory in Christ Jesus. For the righteous shall be recompensed in the earth as I delight in the law of the LORD and meditate day and night in your word. So, I shall be like a tree planted by the rivers of water, that brings forth its fruit in its season, whose leaf also shall not wither; and whatever I do shall prosper. For the LORD God is my sun and shield and will give me grace and glory so no good thing will be withheld from me. I declare your word over my life and rebuke and renounce the spirits of poverty, anti-progress, delay, hinderance, limitation, and backwardness over my life. In Jesus' might name, I pray, Amen.

Actionable Steps:

If you are not financially able to donate, can you cook a meal for someone not able to cook for themselves, give someone a ride, or give clothes to the needy? Can you babysit for someone to alleviate the burden of childcare costs? These are just some of the ways that you can bless others. As a reminder, do not brag or tell anyone what you are doing for you want to be rewarded by God, not man, as in Matthew 6:4.

LESS "PRIDE" & MORE HUMBLENESS

Arrogance Ego Haughty Levithan Perfectionism Pride

Pride is having a holier-than-thou attitude of oneself in comparison with others. Don't allow the praises of men keep you from directing glory to God, for you will think too highly of yourself and thereby believe you are a God.

Scriptures:

"Proud and haughty scorner is his name, who dealeth in proud wrath." (Proverbs 21:24)

"If my people, which are called by my name, shall humble themselves, and pray, and seek my face, and turn from their wicked ways; then will I hear from heaven, and will forgive their sin, and will heal their land." (2 Chronicles 7:14-22)

"Humble yourselves in the sight of the LORD, and he shall lift you up." (James 4:10)

"Likewise, ye younger, submit yourselves unto the elder. Yea, all of you be subject one to another, and be clothed with humility: for God resisteth the proud, and giveth grace to the humble. Humble yourselves therefore under the mighty hand of God, that he may exalt you in due time." (1 Peter 5:5-6)

"For whosoever exalteth himself shall be abased; and he that humbleth himself shall be exalted." (Luke 14:11)

"The fear of the LORD is the instruction of wisdom; and before honour is humility." (Proverbs 15:33)

"Only by pride cometh contention: but with the well advised is wisdom." (Proverbs 13:10)

"And all these blessings shall come on thee, and overtake thee, if thou shalt hearken unto the voice of the LORD thy God." (Deuteronomy 28:2)

Actionable Steps:

Make it a habit to always give praise to God regardless of how you feel or what you are facing at the current time. The enemy wants you to withhold praise or get mad at God when you are in a particular situation. The enemy wants you to complain and speak negatively about the situation so he can keep you there longer. Try to keep an atmosphere of praise for praise can make God changed his mind about you.

I will praise you, LORD, with all my heart;
I will tell of all the marvelous things you have done.
I will be filled with joy because of you.
I will sing praises to your name, O Most High.
(Psalm 9 NLT)

MERRY-GO-ROUND OF UNFORGIVENESS

Offense - Disappointment - Resentment - Unforgiveness

Years of unforgiveness creates sicknesses and infirmities in the body.

This is one of the most difficult sins to try to overcome, especially when the person continues to wrong you. I had to forgive people who sexually assaulted me, blocked job promotions, falsely accused and spread lies about me, in addition to using witchcraft and sorcery on me. Just seeing or hearing their names brought up rage in me. I questioned God a lot about why he did not stop this from happening. I know the enemy can't do anything without his approval. Why are they getting blessed tremendously and they are wicked people? Why am I not receiving a huge breakthrough when I at least try to live my life right? I prayed several times asking God what sin I am still committing that I have not repenting from or still partaking in that causing my enemies to be able to afflict me. The LORD said unforgiveness!

Scriptures:

"If I had cherished sin in my heart, the LORD would not have listened." (Psalm 66:18 NLT)

"But there is forgiveness with thee, that thou mayest be feared." (Psalm 130:4)

"But he that shall blaspheme against the Holy Ghost hath never forgiveness but is in danger of eternal damnation." Mark 3:29)

"Him hath God exalted with his right hand to be a Prince and a Saviour, for to give repentance to Israel, and forgiveness of sins." (Acts 5:31)

"Be it known unto you therefore, men and brethren, that through this man is preached unto you the forgiveness of sins" (Acts 13:38)

"To open their eyes, and to turn them from darkness to light, and from the power of Satan unto God, that they may receive forgiveness of sins, and inheritance among them which are sanctified by faith that is in me." (Acts 26:18)

"In whom we have redemption through his blood, the forgiveness of sins, according to the riches of his grace." (Ephesians 1:7)

"For if ye forgive men their trespasses, your heavenly Father will also forgive you." (Matthew 6:14)

"But I say unto you, love your enemies, bless them that curse you, do good to them that hate you, and pray for them which despitefully use you, and persecute you." (Matthew 5:44)

"He will turn again, he will have compassion upon us; he will subdue our iniquities; and thou wilt cast all their sins into the depths of the sea." (Micah 7:19)

Prayer Point:

Father God, I pray for forgiveness for allowing bitterness, disappointment, unforgiveness, and resentment to reign in my life. I pray for help to remove hatred in my heart, let it be cast into the depths of the sea like you subdue my iniquities according to Micah 7:19. I am asking for full repentance and to be loose from these spirts as well as the spirt of infirmity in Ephesians 1:7. For I am redeemed through the blood of Jesus Christ according to the riches of his grace. Father God, I ask for these sinful doors to be permanently sealed shut with his almighty blood, in Jesus's mighty name I pray, Amen.

Actionable Steps:

Before you go to bed, start thinking about the series of events that happened throughout the day. Did you lose your temper, use profanity, commit adultery, lie, gossip, etc.? Next, think about how you should have handled the situation and what can be done next time to keep you from sinning. Always repent and ask God for forgiveness of your sins as well as put on your full spiritual armor by declaring Ephesian 6:13-18 before going to sleep. If you need an example of true forgiveness, read Genesis 37- 45. You don't have to have a relationship with them but do not speak any evil towards them. If it's your parent or siblings, it's recommended to at least get back on speaking terms. Stop reading this book and call them, if they do not answer leave a voice message saying I was just thinking about you, and I just wanted to say I love you. If they don't respond or still do not want to communicate with you, then you have done your part in taking the first step to forgiveness.

WITCHCRAFT IS YOUR ENTERTAINMENT

Witchcraft is not only casting spells while utilizing sorcery and divination.

Witchcraft = Manipulation + Deception + Domination

Astrology Black/White Magic Burning Sage Crystals
Eastern Star Fortune Telling Fraternities Herbalist
Horoscopes Hypnosis Karate Law of Attraction
Freemason Martial Arts Meditation Mediums
New Age Numerology Occult Ouija
Board Sororities Superstition Tarot Cards Telepathy
Twerking Video Games Voodoo Yoga Zumba

Do you read your horoscope, brag about your astrology sign, and take surveys regarding what spirit animal you are? Well, whatever entertains you, you agree with it. The devil uses this as his opportunity to impose curses against you and to stop you from fulfilling your purpose. The enemy's tactics involve planting seeds, which represent thoughts or negative ideas. These seeds are pervasive, aiming to infiltrate unprotected minds or vessels. A vivid imagination can unwittingly nurture these seeds if not challenged. Belief acts as a gateway to the spirit and represents an agreement with thoughts. For if a seed goes unchallenged, it will grow and take root.

Scriptures:

"Thou art wearied in the multitude of thy counsels. Let now the astrologers, the stargazers, the monthly prognosticators, stand up, and save thee from these things that shall come upon thee. Behold, they shall be as stubble; the fire shall burn them; they shall not deliver themselves from the power of the flame: there shall not be a coal to warm at, nor fire to sit before it." (Isaiah 47:13-14)

"There shall not be found among you anyone that maketh his son or his daughter to pass through the fire, or that useth divination, or an observer of times, or an enchanter, or a witch. Or a charmer, or a consulter with familiar spirits, or a wizard, or a necromancer. For all that do these things are an abomination unto the LORD: and because of these abominations the LORD thy God doth drive them out from before thee." (Deuteronomy 18:10-12)

"And when they shall say unto you, seek unto them that have familiar spirits, and unto wizards that peep, and that mutter: should not a people seek unto their God? for the living to the dead?" (Isaiah 8:19)

Prayer Point:

Father God, I believe Jesus Christ died on the cross and through him I ask for forgiveness for ____________, ____________, ____________ I am redeemed through his innocent blood. I pray that I am led by the Holy Spirt as I seek to build my relationship with you. I renounce and rebuke all covenants with Satan's kingdom, and I declare my body is the temple of the Holy Ghost for I was bought with a price. Father, let the blood of Jesus purify and cleanse my mind, body, soul, and spirit as I declare your word in Jeremiah 29:11 that your thoughts for me are to provide me with peace and an expected end. In Jesus' mighty name, I pray. Amen

(IN THE SPACE, ANNOUNCE YOUR SINS)

Actionable Steps:

After participating in any of the activities listed on this page, list what feelings you have afterwards? How is your mood? Do you feel like committing a sin? Do you think Jesus will approve of the idol worship and participation in witchcraft? Renounce and repent if you decide to give these things up to glorify God, fast to break the stronghold, and get rid of all items associated with it.

MAINTAINING YOUR DELIVERANCE

When something bad is happening in your life, it could be because of one or more reason 1) You violated God's commandment or law (Deuteronomy 28:15); 2) Someone is working witchcraft against you; 3) There is a generational curse; 4) God wants you to grow stronger and learn his laws.

"Ye shall know them by their fruits. Do men gather grapes of thorns, or figs of thistles?" (Matthew 7:16)

Look at your leaders' lives. Are their children blessed and living righteously? Do they gossip and always ask for tithing? Do they belong to a fraternity, sorority, free masonry, or occult? Are the members of the church receiving deliverance or is the church full of people with cancer, diabetes, high blood pressure, fornicators, adulterers, or poverty-stricken individuals?

"Beloved, believe not every spirit, but try the spirits whether they are of God: because **many false prophets are gone out into the world**." (1 John 4:1)

To maintain deliverance, read the Bible, pray, listen to praise and worship music, try to do the right thing, cast negative thoughts into captivity, stop fornicating, confess and repent your sins and fast often.

"But the fearful, and unbelieving, and the abominable, and **murderers**, and whoremongers, and sorcerers, and idolaters, and all liars, shall have their part in the lake which burneth with fire and brimstone: which is the second death." (Revelation 21:8)

__Abortion__ is considered murdered in God's eyes, you must repent from committing murder

Scriptures:

"Call to me and I will answer you and tell you great and unsearchable things you do not know." (Jeremiah 33:3)

"For God so loved the world, that he gave his only begotten Son, that whosoever believeth in him should not perish, but have everlasting life." (John 3:16)

"But He answered and said, "It is written, 'Man shall not live by bread alone, but by every word that proceeds from the mouth of God." (Matthew 4:4)

"So, then faith cometh by hearing, and hearing by the word of God." (Romans 10:17)

"For I am the LORD: I will speak, and the word that I shall speak shall come to pass; it shall be no more prolonged: for in your days, O rebellious house, will I say the word, and will perform it, saith the LORD God." (Ezekiel 12:25)

"And whatsoever ye shall ask in my name, that will I do, that the Father may be glorified in the Son. If ye shall ask anything in my name, I will do it. If ye love me, keep my commandments." (John 14:13-15)

"Jesus came to fulfill the law and release the Spirit of grace to live in man. For by grace are ye saved through faith; and that not of yourselves: it is the gift of God." (Ephesians 2:8)

"And thou shalt love the LORD thy God with all thine heart, and with all thy soul, and with all thy might." (Deuteronomy 6:5)

"Be not deceived: evil communications corrupt good manners." (1 Corinthians 15:33)

"Delight thyself also in the LORD: and he shall give thee the desires of thine heart." (Psalm 37:4)

"I am crucified with Christ: nevertheless, I live; yet not I, but Christ liveth in me: and the life which I now live in the flesh I live by the faith of the Son of God, who loved me, and gave himself for me." (Galatians 2:20)

"But seek ye first the kingdom of God, and his righteousness; and all these things shall be added unto you." (Matthew 6:33)

"People who conceal their sins will not prosper, but if they confess and turn from them, they will receive mercy." (Proverbs 28:13)

"The LORD is my strength and my shield; my heart trusted in him, and I am helped: therefore, my heart greatly rejoiceth; and with my song will I praise him." (Psalm 28:7)

"I can do all things through Christ which strengtheneth me." (Philippians 4:13)

"Be careful for nothing; but in everything by prayer and supplication with thanksgiving let your requests be made known unto God." (Philippians 4:6)

"The LORD is far from the wicked: but he heareth the prayer of the righteous." (Proverbs 15:29)

"If we confess our sins, he is faithful and just to forgive us our sins, and to cleanse us from all unrighteousness." (1 John 1:9)

Prayer Point:

Jehovah, I cancel and break the covenant that will give any spirit any right to re-enter my life. I cancel any covenant or agreement that will work against me, I reject and renounce it right now. I divorce myself from every evil spirit that feels it has the right to re-enter my life through my cooperation. For the LORD is my strength and my shield; my heart trusted in him, and I am helped. In Jesus' name I declare, Amen.

Actionable Steps:

1) Be mindful there is a holy and demonic tongue. Do not let anyone speak in tongues over you.
2) Avoid conversation regarding your past because you will

start reminiscing and may backslide. Don't resurrect what you have already killed.

3) Keep your household cleansed and dedicated to the LORD. Be mindful of what you watch and bring into your house.
4) Always pray over your food and drink. Be mindful of where and who you receive food from. In addition, throw away gifts received from coworkers or associates especially pens, jewelry, perfume, or shoes. There are more people practicing witchcraft than you ever know, including the Christian* witch.
5) Try not to make big decisions without fasting and praying. The devil wants to wear out the Saints. Your breakthrough is in your worship. Don't focus on the problem; focus on God's word.
6) Practice yielding to the Holy Spirit to avoid sinning. Don't do it on your own strength.
7) Declare blessing over your life by adding verses from Deuteronomy 28:1-13 in your prayers.
8) Don't go to sleep or leave the house without applying the blood of Jesus Christ. (Psalm 91 & Ephesians 6:11-17)
9) Evil spirits transfer to those who are not living their life right. The same thing applies when it comes to praying for others. Those who are called to be intercessors, need to try to live a life of repentance and fasting. As a reminder, evil communication corrupts good manners. (Matthew 17:21 and 1 Corinthians 15:33)
10) Lastly, spread the gospel. What an honor it is to help bring people to the Kingdom of Light!

***Reminder**: In the spirit realm is where everything is conceived, if you do not challenge your dreams through prayer and fasting, then, by default, you're in agreement, and you will watch these things play out in your physical life.*

With faith, say your prayers with 3 or more applicable scriptures, giving thanks to God afterwards

Recommendations to Increase Your Spiritual Growth

Books

Bible-Based Dictionary by Dr. Joe Ibojie
Conquer Your Deliverance by John Ramirez
Demon Hit List by John Eckhardt
Discerning the Spirit Realm by Rebecca Greenwood
Fire Prayers by John Ramirez
He Came to Set the Captives Free by Rebecca Brown, MD
*King James Version of the Holy Bible
Overthrowing Evil Altars by Uzor Ndekwu
Prayers that Rout Demons by John Eckhardt
*Prayers that Work by Kevin LA Ewing
Prepare for War by Rebecca Brown, MD
*The Bible Promise Book by Barbour Publishing

Websites

kevinlaewing.blogspot.com

stephendarbyministries.com (partnership access)

Youtube

Derek Prince
Kevin LA Ewing
Stephanie Ike Okafor
Stephen Darby Ministries

About the Author

Lafietta Christian is a retired professional with a wealth of experience spanning over 25 years. With a Master's degree in Education, Ms. Christian spent two decades as an educator, mentor, and coach, facilitating growth and development in individuals of all ages. Having also accumulated 20 years of expertise in the finance industry, Ms. Christian brings a unique perspective to personal and professional growth.

A proud native of Montgomery, Alabama, Ms. Christian is deeply devoted to living a life centered around faith in Jesus Christ. This unwavering commitment guides her vision of providing counseling and support for those facing mental health challenges, including depression, anxiety, and other life struggles. Her heart is to empower others to overcome adversity, find hope, and lead fulfilling lives.

Ms. Lafietta Christian combines her diverse career experiences and passion for service to inspire and uplift those in need, with the hope of making a lasting impact in the world.

Made in the USA
Columbia, SC
09 January 2025